Walking in Faith

Doug Roberts

Walking in Faith

by Doug Roberts

Published by:

> *Doug Roberts Publishing*
> *P. O. Box 321*
> *Frederick, Oklahoma 73542*

Printed in the United States of America

ISBN: 978-0-9825992-4-2

I thank Ed Chinn, Tim and Laurie Thornton, and Shellie Kushnerick for all the work they did helping me transfer the things in my heart into print.

Table of Contents

Chapter 1: Knowing Who You Are

For whatever is born of God overcomes the world; and this is the victory that has overcome the world—our faith.
Who is the one who overcomes the world, but he who believes that Jesus is the Son of God?
—1John 5:4-5

Does this verse tell us that He who overcomes the world is the one that believes that Jesus is the Son of God? I don't think so. The devil believes that Jesus is the Son of God.

Our faith, or our belief that Jesus was and is the Son of God, is what overcomes the world. For Jesus to be Son means that He has to have a Father, and because Jesus is a faithful Son, He also brings many other sons to the Father and gives them access to the Father (Hebrews 2:10). They can also be sons who walk in that which God has predestined for them. What overcomes the world is our belief in who we are as sons in the Father's house. As He was on the earth, now we are on the earth (1 John 4:17).

What about Sin?

Do you know that Jesus could have sinned? He walked this earth as a man just like I am. He could have sinned, but He chose not to sin because He would not dishonor His Father and because

He wanted to fulfill the requirements that the Father had for him. What keeps me from sinning is not the fear of hell; it is that I don't want to dishonor my Father. Sinning violates everything that's in me.

For me to sin, I would have to go against everything that I am and everything I believe. That's just too hard. I'd rather not sin. Things that used to be a temptation to me are not even a distraction now. Why? Because I'm growing in the fullness of who God's called me to be.

> What keeps me from sinning is not the fear of hell; it is that I don't want to dishonor my Father. Sinning violates everything that's in me.

We have the ability to sin. We have the ability to do stupid things. What keeps us from that is our love for the Father. We want to bring honor to Him just like Jesus did. How? By being obedient to the Father. That is what overcomes the world—our faith in believing in who we are as sons.

"That's Not Who I Am Anymore"

Let me tell you part of my story. In 1974, I got saved and filled with the Holy Spirit. At that time, I had a big drug habit. When I got saved God delivered me from drugs. About a week after I got delivered, I went over to my brother's house. He was still dealing drugs. When I arrived at his house, there was a pound of marijuana on the table. People were all over the house doing drugs. I didn't I didn't need that anymore because I had found out who I was in Christ. know that was going on when I walked in. They said, "Hey, Doug! Come join the party."

But when I looked around, the Spirit of the Lord spoke to me: "That's not who you are any more and you don't need that."

So I told them, that's not who I am anymore and I don't need that."

I didn't need that anymore because I had found out who I was in Christ and that what Christ had for me was all the blessings of the Father, which are eternal.

Chapter 2: Victory over the Enemy

And I give eternal life to them, and they shall never perish; and no one will snatch them out of My hand. My Father, who has given them to Me, is greater than all; and no one is able to snatch them out of the Father's hand.
— John 10:28-29

Do you know what one of the promises of God is to you? Eternal life. When you accept Jesus as your Lord and Savior, you're not temporal anymore. You become eternal. You will never perish. Why? Because in Christ, you're eternal. Jesus told us, "My Father who has given them to Me, is greater than all, and no one is able to snatch them out of the Father's hand" (John 10:29).

This is who you are. It's who we are. If we ever really understand and walk in that, then the devil is defeated.

When No Weapon Formed Against You Will Stand

> The devil knows that when you know who you are, no weapon formed against you will prosper.

Does the devil know your name? Some of you may say, "I don't want the devil to know my name!" Well, I sure want the devil to know my name! Why? Because when the Jewish exorcists tried to cast out a demon in Acts 19, the demon said that it knew Jesus and Paul, but it didn't know the exorcists. Then the demon beat them up and they ran out of the house naked.

When the devil knows your name, he knows *you* also know your name. He also knows that when you know who you are, no weapon formed against you will prosper. No plan set against you can succeed. Greater is He who is in you than He who opposes you. So when the devil knows your name, he knows he's already defeated.

That's why the devil always tries to minister to us through fear, through accusation, and through deception. He tries to make us believe lies so that we won't walk in the truth of who we are. The devil tries to put our identity in things we do instead of in who we are as sons and daughters of the Lord.

How to Get Beyond Stupid

I've done stupid things and when I sin, the devil says to me, "Look who you are. You're not really who you say you are. Look what you did."

But then the Holy Spirit says, "What did you do?"

"I did a stupid thing, Lord."

5

And Jesus says, "I forgive stupid."

And then the Father says, "What are you talking about? I just see the blood."

1 John 3:7-8 tells us, "The one who practices righteousness is righteous…the one who practices sin is of the devil."

The devil always tries to keep us in what we were so we won't come into who we are.

We practice righteousness but every now and then the spirit of stupid gets on us, and when that happens, the devil says, "That's who you are." But that's not true! That's just what I *did*. It's not who I *am*. Who I *am* is the righteousness of God in Christ Jesus.

Remember, the Holy Spirit convicts us, Jesus forgives us, and God just says, "That's my son/daughter." The devil will always try to keep us in what we were so we won't come into who we are. The devil always tries to keep us in the temporal things so we'll lose sight of the eternal things.

Chapter 3: Afflictions Help Us to See

And we know that God causes all things to work together for good to those who love God, to those who are called according to His purpose.

—Romans 8:28

The scriptures tell us that we enter the Kingdom of God through much tribulation. When I'm in tribulation, I know it's working for my good because I know that *all things* work together for my good. In those times my prayer is, "Lord, let me see what is good in this tribulation so I can focus on that and get on with the journey, because this is temporary."

Paul said these momentary, light afflictions—which for him were being shipwrecked, bitten by a snake, stoned, and

> We've got to get our minds renewed so that when we find ourselves in momentary and light affliction, we realize it's only temporal and we don't lose sight of the eternal.

forsaken by all of Asia—have nothing to do with the eternal. We've got to get our minds renewed so that when we find ourselves in a momentary and light affliction, we realize it's only temporal, meaning earthly or material, and we don't lose sight of the eternal.

The Purpose of His Discipline

God disciplines us because we're sons and daughters. He does not discipline His children out of anger but rather because He wants us to be more like Him. Every parent understands this. When children keep going down a dangerous road, do we just let them go? No! We discipline them and bring them back. Why? Because we love them. God loves us so much that He chastens us, He disciplines us, and He encourages us. He does so because He is a father. He loves us.

When we find ourselves in a difficult situation, it doesn't mean God doesn't love us. In fact, it means exactly the opposite. God loves us! Our afflictions cause us to become more like Him! Remember, even Jesus "learned obedience from the things which He suffered" (Hebrews 5:8).

Chapter 4: His Strength vs. Our Strength

Years ago, after making some bad investments, I decided to return to farming to ease our financial burden. I thought surely the money I could make would make everything okay. After all, as I explained to everyone, "I'm a good farmer. I will do just fine." I planted my cotton crop, and it was a very good cotton crop. Just before I started to harvest it, though, a hail storm came and wiped it out.

I thought that was a little strange, but I was still sure everything would be okay. After all, I still had my cattle, so I started to get my cattle ready to sell. Before I sold them, though, they started dropping dead.

I thought that was really strange, but I still had my wheat operation. Right before I started cutting the wheat, another hail storm destroyed my wheat crop. That stopped me cold.

I said, "God, what is happening?" You know what He told me?

He said, "I just wanted to show you what you could do."

And then I remembered my foolish statement: "I'm a good farmer; I will do just fine."

That's when God spoke to me from Jeremiah 17:5-8,

Thus says the Lord,

"Cursed is the man who trusts in mankind

And makes flesh his strength,

And whose heart turns away from the Lord.

For he will be like a bush in the desert

And will not see when prosperity comes,

But will live in stony wastes in the wilderness,

A land of salt without inhabitant.

Blessed is the man who trusts in the Lord

And whose trust is the Lord.

For he will be like a tree planted by the water,

That extends its roots by a stream

And will not fear when the heat comes;

But its leaves will be green,

And it will not be anxious in a year of drought

Nor cease to yield fruit."

Trusting in What I Could Do

Things were going fine in the ministry because I knew I couldn't do ministry; that had to be God. But in farming, I was a good farmer, so I could trust in my ability.

The Lord nailed me that day: "Cursed is the man who trusts in mankind and makes flesh his strength,

10

and whose heart turns away from the Lord." When all this was happening, I was still ministering the Gospel. People were getting saved and baptized in the Holy Ghost. God was blessing my ministry, but in my farming I trusted in my flesh. I trusted in what I could do, and as a result, everything just fell apart.

Things were going fine in the ministry because I knew I couldn't *do* ministry. That had to be God. However, I was a good farmer so I could trust in my ability. In that, my heart had turned away from the Lord. It wasn't that I was in sin. It wasn't that I had fallen away from God. But in my heart I had said, "God, I really don't need you in this. I can do it." That's when God said, "I just wanted to show you what you could do."

Allowing Him to be Our Trust

I thank God for verse 7: "But blessed is the man who trusts in the Lord and whose trust is the Lord." It's one thing to trust the Lord, but it's another thing to allow the Lord to be your trust. I no longer just trust the Lord; He *is* my trust! It's in Him that I live and move. I can do nothing without Him. I believe that. I know what I'm capable of in the flesh: death. I know what He's capable of: life.

When the Lord becomes our trust we can be like a tree planted by the water that extends its roots by the streams. We will not fear when the heat comes. Our leaves will be green, we'll not be anxious in the year of drought, and we'll never cease yielding fruit. That is Kingdom life.

What you can accomplish in your flesh is death. What He can accomplish in you is endless and incredible. Never forget that you're nothing outside of Christ.

Chapter 5: He Will Do What He Must

Do you remember the story of Jesus riding into Jerusalem on a donkey as the people shouted, "Hosanna! Hosanna!"? Now, just imagine what that donkey was thinking as multitudes laid palm leaves on the ground as he walked past: "Man, I never had this kind of celebration before!"

It wasn't about the donkey! It was about the One riding the donkey. It's not about you, either; it's about Christ in you! Christ in you is the hope of glory. Think of it. He chose you, He called you, and He appointed you to be the donkey!

> It wasn't about the donkey, it was about the One riding the donkey.

God is going to do what He has to do. Remember, His purposes are not about you, but about Him in you. So if God does great things, realize it's really not about, through, or even for you. If God doesn't do anything, realize that that's not on your shoulders, either. For example, many people have been raised from the dead through prayer. However, I have prayed for people and they died. Hallelujah! It's not about me! It's about Him in me. If you pray for someone and they die, realize they're still healed because they're in heaven. That's the way I have to look at it. On the other hand, I've prayed for people and they got healed.

13

Whether they live or die is up to Him, not me and not you. It's all up to Him. It's not about you. Your trust has to be Him.

Fall on the Rock

Years ago God spoke to me and said, "I want you to have faith in who I am. I want you to have more faith in Me being God than in you being able to hear Me." I have faith that God is God, and because He's God He can do what He has to do in my life to get my attention. And He's been faithful in that.

Sometimes He speaks to me and I turn. Sometimes He kind of directs me and I turn. Sometimes He kicks me in the rear and I turn. He is God, and I have found that it's a lot easier to fall on the rock than for the rock to fall on me.

Here's what I mean: Get two clay flower pots. Place a rock on the ground and drop one of the flower pots on the rock. You already know that it will break into pieces, but they will be big enough that you can pick them up and put them back together.

Now take that other pot, put it on the ground, and drop the rock on it. You'll see there are no pieces large enough to put back together. So like I said, it's better to fall on the rock than to have the rock fall on you.

God loves us so much that He will do whatever He has to do to fulfill his purpose in our lives. He's our Father and we're His sons. He has a plan and a purpose for us. These little momentary, light afflictions are working for our good so that we'll be like Him. In 43 years of walking with the Lord, I've learned how to listen better. That's not because I'm so spiritual; it's because I'd much rather hear the voice of the Lord than receive the kick of the Lord. They both work for my good, but I like the voice better than the kick.

> These little momentary, light afflictions are working for our good so that we'll be like Him.

Chapter 6: Get Your Mind Renewed

By this the love of God was manifested in us, that God has sent His only begotten Son into the world so that we might live through Him. In this is love, not that we loved God, but that He loved us and sent His Son to be the propitiation for our sins.

—1 John 4:9-10

How do we live in the world? According to the above scripture, we live in the world through Christ. We have no life outside of the life we have in Christ. He loved us while we weren't even loving Him, and He wants us to live in Christ. We've got to get our minds renewed if we are going to do that.

Let's look at Colossians 3:1-4: "If then you have been raised up with Christ, keep seeking the things above, where Christ is, seated at the right hand of God. Set your mind on the things above, not on the things that are on earth. For you have died and your life is hidden with Christ in God. When Christ, who is our life, is revealed, then you also will be revealed with Him in glory."

The Age to Come

Christ is being revealed on the earth now through us. That's why we seek the things above, not the things of the earth. Several scriptures refer to "this present age" and "the age to come." What do these two terms mean? Think about two paper plates. The first plate represents the age that we live in, or this present age. The other plate represents the age that is coming. That age, or the age to come, is all about God in the fullness of His glory, when the earth will be fully and manifestly His.

Currently we're in this present age—the first plate—but we encounter Jesus, who is of the age **We're of the age that is coming, which is the fullness of God, and His full authority and His full Kingdom. That's who we** to come. Even though we are living in this present age, the more we behold Him and come into our identity in Christ, the more the age to come invades, like one plate moving over the other (see the illustration below).

Miraculously, we can get to a place where we're living in the fullness of the age that is coming, but doing so right in this present age. That's why the scripture says, "We're in the world, but we're not of the world" and that we are "aliens" in this present age. We're simultaneously here in the present age and living in and by the power of the age to come.

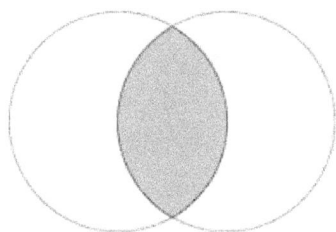

We're of the age that is coming, which is the fullness of God, His full authority and His full Kingdom. That's who we are.

Therefore, in this present age, we can declare the age that is coming because the fullness of God lives in us. This is the faith that overcomes the world. This is who we are. This is the authority that's been given to us.

Chapter 7: He Will Align Your Condition with Your Position

Therefore we do not lose heart, but though our outer man is decaying, yet our inner man is being renewed day by day. For momentary, light affliction is producing for us an eternal weight of glory far beyond all comparison, while we look not at the things which are seen, but at the things which are not seen; for the things which are seen are temporal, but the things which are not seen are eternal.

— 2 Corinthians 4:16-18

We don't look to the things which are seen; we look to the things which are *not* seen, all found in Christ. The world cannot see the unseen things. It cannot even understand them because it doesn't know God or the Holy Spirit.

But we do, so we are His children. The world cannot even see us. This is how you can do the things God has predestined you to do in Christ: You're looking at the things which are unseen by man.

Hebrews 11:1 says, "Faith is the assurance of things hoped for, the conviction of things not seen." I have a conviction of the things that are not seen. Why? Because I'm in Christ and I know the work is finished. I'm calling out of eternity—remember, the age to come—that which is finished and I'm declaring it into this present age. Do you understand?

The Difference between Our Position and Our Condition

No one has full understanding. That's why we need the Holy Spirit. He gives us understanding and teaches us. Part of his job is to bring revelation of the unseen.

We all need to understand that our eternal position in God is firm, established, and unshakeable. Our condition, however, is a separate, temporal, and sometimes fragile thing. Our position is that we are seated in heavenly places in Christ Jesus. Our condition is sometimes very different. That's why we don't look at our condition. We look to our position until our condition lines up with our position.

In your condition, ask Him for whatever you need that will help you line up with your eternal position. Ask Him and He'll do it.

> We look to our position until our condition lines up with our position.

He will do it because He knows your position. He knows who you are, the works He's called you to do, and it gives Him joy to help align your temporal condition on earth with your eternal position in Heaven.

20

What are the things in life that are temporal? Take an example from Genesis. Ishmael was temporal, and God blessed him. Isaac, however, was eternal. He received the blessing, but he was part of God's covenant. Many times we settle for the blessing and never get the covenant. You can have a blessing without a covenant, though when you get the covenant, you also get all the blessings.

> If heaven was God's ultimate purpose for us, then when we accepted Jesus, why didn't the Father just send us on to heaven?

We're not Ishmaels, we're Isaacs—men and women of the covenant. The Law is temporal; the Promise is eternal. The flesh is temporal; the Spirit is eternal. Traditions taught by man are temporal; revelation taught by the Spirit is eternal. Religion is temporal; relationships are eternal.

What Is Our Inheritance?

We need to get our minds off of just hoping we go to heaven. Heaven is not our goal. If heaven was God's ultimate purpose for us, then when we accepted Jesus why wouldn't He just send us on to heaven?

No, God's promise to Abraham and his descendants was and is that they would inherit the earth. Did you know that we are included in this promise? The earth is our inheritance. Why is it our inheritance? Because God wants us to rule and reign and establish His purposes on it.

I think the Lord wants us to get our minds off of going to heaven and become *doers* here on earth. If you inherited a large ranch, would you want to walk away from it? Wouldn't you become a doer? Wouldn't you raise livestock, plant crops, build barns, fix fences, buy equipment, and study the markets so that your land would prosper?

We are people of the promise; we have the Holy Spirit. The world does not know or understand the Holy Spirit, and so it doesn't know or understand us, either. The world is never going to be happy with us, so let's quit trying to please the world. Remember the earth is waiting for us to come into our identity as sons and daughters of God, to declare the things of God, and to see the fullness of the age that is coming. Be who you *are*.

The earth is waiting for you to come into your identity as sons and daughters of God, to declare the things of God, and to see the fullness of the age that is coming.

When you understand who you are, things change. It doesn't matter where your home is; what matters is your position in Christ. I live in Frederick, Oklahoma but if I am in China, I'm going to prosper because I live in Christ. If I am in Mexico, I'm going to prosper because I live in Christ. The Kingdom of God is not greater in the United States than it is in Mexico. It's not greater in China than it is in Africa. There's just one Kingdom of God. There's just one Jesus. There's just one Holy Spirit. God chose you, He called you, He appointed you, and now you can begin to understand why He called you. You can know what your job is.

God is for you. What or who can be against you?

My heart's desire is for you is to be all that God's called you to be. But how are you going to be that if you don't know what it is? Coming to a meeting, praising Jesus, putting some money in a bucket is such a small part of what the Father has called you to. Raise your vision, take ownership of the grace of Christ that's in you, and proclaim the word of the Lord and watch what God will do.

Group Discussion Guide

My hope and purpose for this book is to see it become seed in the rich soil of human hearts. These questions were put together by some brothers and sisters to help you work these truths into your life.

1. Jesus is the eternal Son of God and He made a way for us to enter into a son/daughter relationship with the Father, though many live as though they still need to perform some religious or heroic deeds in order to be secure in their relationship with the Lord. Why do you think this is?

2. Why do you think Jesus lived a sinless life when He walked the earth?

3. I stopped living in sin because I came to see that that was not who I was in Christ. How does your identity in Christ shape the way you live?

4. There is a distinction between who we are and what we do—we are righteous but we sometimes we sin. When we do sin, it does not change who we are. Is that distinction helpful to you? Does it give you greater victory over sin? If so, how?

5. Hebrews 5:8 tells us that "Jesus learned obedience by the things which He suffered." How do real life afflictions serve the eternal purposes of God? How have you seen this to be true in your own life?

6. Think back to the story about how I trusted God in ministry vs. how I trusted Him in farming, Can you recall a time in your own life when you placed your trust in something other than in Him?

7. What does it mean for the Lord to be your trust?

8. The world focuses a great deal on individuality: It's all about ME. Do you think that way of thinking undermines our relationship with God? What would it mean to have our minds renewed in that area?

9. Do you see how this present age and the age to come are sometimes simultaneously happening? Which of these two is your default mode? What would it look like if the age to come were your default? Is that possible before we die? How?

10. What is the difference between your eternal position and your earthly condition? How can we best bring our condition into agreement and alignment with our position?

11. What does it mean that in Christ you are an Isaac and not an Ishmael?

12. Do you have an eternal inheritance? What is it?

www.ingramcontent.com/pod-product-compliance
Lightning Source LLC
Chambersburg PA
CBHW020449030426
42337CB00014B/1472